free with no Stamp
from School.

REALLY COOL
Magic Card TRICKS

Created & written by the Top That!™ team
Designed by Top That! and The Visual Works

TOP THAT!™

Published by Top That! Publishing
Tide Mill Way, Woodbridge, Suffolk, IP12 1AP, UK
www.topthatpublishing.com

CONTENTS

2

SECRETS OF SUCCESS

For centuries people have been fascinated by magic. Magic is on TV, in theatres, at parties; magic has its own clubs, societies, books and famous people. Get to grips with the tricks in this book, and before you know it, you'll be finding chosen cards, using telepathy, and mind reading!

But before you can become an ace magician and carry out these amazing feats, there are a few golden rules, handy hints and tricks of the trade which you need to know…

Perfect Performance

There's a lot more to magic than just doing each trick. You need to perform it! Whether there are thousands of people in the audience or just the pet cat, every magician is a performer. How successful the performance is will rely not on how difficult each trick is, as most tricks are actually very easy. Instead, it is how the trick is performed that decides whether it will be a success or not. Create an illusion: give yourself a stage name such as 'The Astounding Astro' or 'Marvellous Melvyn the Mystical'. Put together a simple stage costume – wear clothes of all the same colour for a dramatic effect, or go for the traditional look with white gloves and a top hat.

Perfect Patter

This is really important! If you draw your audience into your performance with some really slick chat, you will divert their attention from what you are doing with your hands!

Smile at them and include lines such as 'Here's a trick that's just a little bit different…' or 'Now this trick is just unbelievable…'. Humour can also be used to great effect as the audience will find it more difficult to see what you are doing if they are laughing. Never perform the same trick twice in front of the same audience. You don't want them to guess your secrets!

Practice, Practice, Practice!

The importance of practice should never be underestimated! It makes the most complicated tricks look effortless, and really boosts your confidence when it's time to perform. As you start to improve you'll be able to attempt more difficult illusions, and can even start creating your own!

Practice is also important when it comes to shuffling the cards. It may take a little while to feel completely comfortable holding a pack of cards and shuffling them between your hands. Make sure you can do this with ease before you perform any of the tricks.

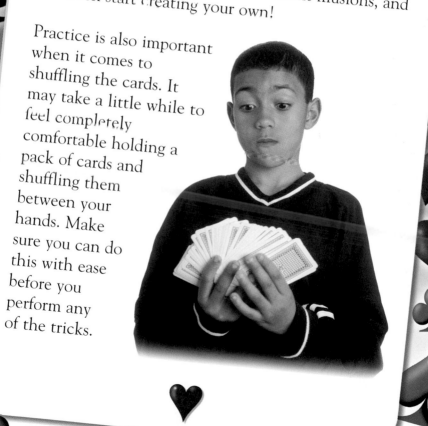

MAGIC MARKED CARDS

This code allows you to identify any card from the deck simply by looking at the reverse.

The cards in this kit may look like ordinary cards, but they have a code marked in the pattern on the back,

in the top left and bottom right corners. You'll need to learn this code well before you can work the trick convincingly. The back of this card tells you it is the five of diamonds.

A mark in one of the code circles tells you the value of the card, starting with the King, Queen and Jack. The numbers follow in descending order, with the Ace on a line of its own. Of course, these letters and numbers are not printed!

Four symbols are used to indicate the suit of the card (heart, club, diamond or spade).

MAGIC TAPERED CARDS

Your second deck of cards is special in a different way. Slide the deck out of the box and hold the cards together firmly. You might be able to see that one end is slightly narrower than the other end.

To see this properly, hold the deck face down in one hand. Cut the cards about halfway down and lift off the top half of the deck. Keeping the cards face down, turn around the top part of the deck for half a turn. Replace it on top of the pack and square up the cards. The wider end of the top cards will stick out from the narrow end of the lower half, ever so slightly.

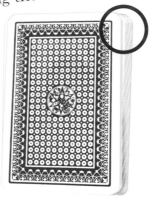

This trickery allows you to identify a single card that has been turned around, just by running your finger and thumb along the edges of the deck. The taper cards are used in many of the tricks in this book, so keep this deck of cards tucked neatly in their box until you need to use them.

On with
the
Show

IS THIS YOUR CARD?

Find your volunteer's card in a deck of 52!

YOU WILL NEED
★ Tapered cards from kit.

1 Shuffle the deck of cards – or, to make the trick even more convincing, allow a volunteer from your audience to do so.

2 Fan out the cards, face down, and offer them to your volunteer. They must now select a card and memorise it.

3 While they are looking at their card, quickly turn the pack around by 180°. This ensures that the thick end of their card will stand out against the thinner ends of the other cards as you feel along the edge of the pack.

4 Ask them to replace the card at any random point in the pack, and shuffle thoroughly. Make sure you don't drop any cards!

5 Now amaze your audience by stripping out your volunteer's card! Amazing!

ACES HIGH

Make the Aces rise to the top of the deck as if by magic!

1 In front of your audience, shuffle through the deck face up and remove all the Aces. Place them on the table so your audience can see them.

YOU WILL NEED
★ Tapered cards from kit.

2 As you gather up the Aces from the table, turn them to face the opposite way to the rest of the cards in the pack. Add aces to the pack and then shuffle the cards.

14

3 Now, holding the cards behind your back, strip out the Aces by how they feel, and one by one, place them at the top of the pack.

4 Place the deck of cards on the desk and tap the top, saying you have made the Aces rise to the top. Lo and behold, when you turn the top four cards over, they will all be Aces!

PRO TIP
Mastering the Taper cards requires lots of practise. Do not use them in your performances until you can strip out the required cards every time.

SURPRISE FOURS

Find a chosen card - and four surprises!

1 Before your performance Turn over a Five and put it on top of the pack. On top of that, put all the Fours, face down.

YOU WILL NEED
★ Any card deck.

2 Ask a member of your audience to choose a card. Put it on the bottom of the pack.

3 Cut the pack, so the chosen card is now next to the top Four.

4 Take each pair of cards from between the fingers and lay them side-by-side face down on the table, making two piles, and saying "Even" each time.

5 Now take the single card. Let your volunteer choose which pile to place it on. Tap both piles and say you will now make the 'odd' card jump from one pile to the other.

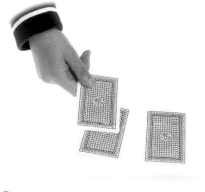

6 Deal out cards from the chosen pile in pairs, saying "Even" each time. Amazingly, it will now be even.

7 Do the same with the other pile, dealing out pairs, and you will be left with one 'odd' card, just as you promised!

COLOUR CODED

YOU WILL NEED
★ Tapered cards from kit.

With all cards face down, separate the red cards from the black!

1 Prepare this trick beforehand, by turning all the red cards in the deck one way, and all the black the other.

2 Fan out the cards evenly, and show the audience that the deck is mixed.

3 While they are looking at the card, casually turn the deck around. They must now replace their chosen card into the deck.

4 You must now use your sleight-of-hand abilities to separate the cards into two face down piles. Pretend you can feel the cards telling you which pile they want to go in. When you turn over the piles, their card will be the only one of an odd colour in the two piles of cards!

ABRACADABRA

A magic spell locates a chosen card.

YOU WILL NEED
★ Any card deck.
★ A volunteer.

1 Deal three piles of cards, face down, until you have seven in each pile. Set aside the rest of the deck.

2 Ask someone to pick one of the piles.

3 Display the chosen cards in a fan to your volunteer. Ask your volunteer to choose a card, but not tell you what it is.

4 Gather up the cards and put the pile containing the chosen card in between the other two piles. Deal the cards in the same way again into three piles of seven.

5 Pick up one pile at a time and display them to the volunteer, asking them to identify the pile which contains their chosen card.

6 Once again, put this pile between the other two and deal out the cards into three piles.

7 Fan out the cards for a third time: ask the volunteer to identify the pile containing their card, then put this pile between the other two.

8 Solemnly spell out the word ABRACADABRA, dealing one card for each of the letters intoned. Turn over the final card to show it is the chosen one!

PRO TIP
This trick only works if you deal three piles at a time, instead of dealing one pile of seven followed by another two piles of seven.

PICK A CARD

An amazing trick you can perform with your magic marked cards.

1 To use your magic marked cards to perform a trick, first shuffle the cards well. Hold them out face down and ask someone to choose one.

2 As the card is removed, casually look for the marking.

3 Ask the person to memorise the card and place it back in the deck.

4 Once the card is replaced, you can stun your audience by announcing which one it was!

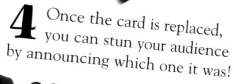

27

TELEPATHY TEST

Demonstrate your baffling telepathic powers!

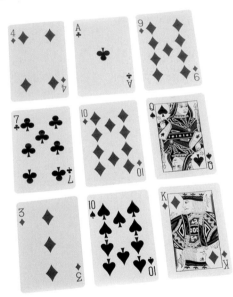

YOU WILL NEED
★ Any card deck.
★ A secret assistant.

1 Shuffle a deck of cards and lay nine cards face up on the table in three rows of three.

2 Give the rest of the pack to a 'volunteer'. Explain you will leave the room for a few moments so the audience can choose one of the cards on the table.

3 Return to the room. Make a play of concentrating, then announce the number chosen. Amazing!

HOW?

Your volunteer must be your secret assistant. Imagine the deck of cards divided into a grid, as shown. The assistant just needs to hold the deck with her thumb on the imaginary square indicating the card chosen.

29

MAGIC SHUFFLE

Magically deal a line of cards in perfect order!

1 Announce you are going to perform a Magic Shuffle. Hold up the cards and show them to be in a 'random' order.

SECRET
You only need ten cards for this trick. Arrange them in advance into:
8, 3, 5, A, 9, 10, 4, 6, 7, 2.

2 Put the first card face down on the table. Put the second card at the bottom of the pack in your hand.

3 Put the third card on top of the one on the table; the fourth at the bottom of the pack. Continue until all the cards are on the table.

4 Pick up the pack and glance through it with dismay. The trick hasn't worked! You forgot to say the magic words.

5 Perform the same shuffle again, but this time saying your magic words.

6 Now deal the cards face up in a line on the table: they will be in perfect order.

GIRL'S BEST FRIEND

Make the diamonds gather together in this sparkling trick!

1 Before you perform the trick, take the suit of diamonds out of the pack and reverse them.

2 You are now ready to perform. Shuffle all the cards thoroughly in front of your audience, saying that you know diamonds are a girl's best friend, and will hand-pick the whole suit, just for them!

3 As you shuffle, discreetly feel along the edges of the cards, stripping out all the diamonds. Place them face-down in a separate pile, until you have them all.

4 Dramatically turn this pile over to reveal all of the diamonds - ta dah!

COUNTING CARDS

Make a chosen card appear at any named point in the deck!

YOU WILL NEED
★ Tapered cards from kit.
★ A Volunteer.

1 Shuffle the deck with the cards all facing the same way, so that they are thoroughly mixed.

2 Allow a volunteer to select a card. Make sure that the card is returned to the pack facing the opposite way to the rest of the cards.

3 Shuffle the cards thoroughly, and hold them behind your back. Strip out the chosen card, and place it on the bottom of the pack.

4 Slide this card back slightly, so that your audience cannot see it. Now ask your volunteer how far they want you to count up the pack to find their card.

5 Slide out the cards from the bottom of the pack but above their chosen one, until you reach the figure they have chosen. Then remove the chosen card and amaze your audience!

THE CHOSEN CARD

A card chosen by a member of your audience is lost in the deck, but you can still find it.

YOU WILL NEED
★ Any card deck.
★ Table.

1 Ask a member of your audience to shuffle a deck of cards. Now take the pack and ask them to select a card and to show the card they have chosen to the rest of the audience.

2 While they are doing this, quickly and secretly look at the card which is on the bottom of the deck.

3 Now divide the deck into two. Put the top half of the cards into your left hand. Ask the member of the audience to replace their chosen card on top of this half, then put the remainder of the cards on top of it.

4 The chosen card will now be below the card that you looked at. To make your trick even more convincing, cut the cards again.

5 Spread the deck of cards face up on a magic table. The card chosen by the member of your audience will be on top of the card which was on the bottom of the deck in step 2.

52 CARD SCATTER

This is a spectacular way to find a chosen card - but it takes nerve!

1 You need to start by losing and then finding a chosen card, (see page 36). Secretly cut the card to the top of the deck.

2 Now ask a member of your audience to hold their hand out, palm upwards. Then position the deck face up in their hand, so that their fingers stretch underneath the cards for at least 2.5 cm and their thumb is on the top of the deck for about 1.5 cm. Ask them to hold the deck firmly.

3 Hold your nerve with this step! Strike down with your hand on the end of the deck which is not being held.

4 All the cards will scatter to the floor, except the chosen card, which is being held firmly between the fingers and thumb of your volunteer.

FLIPPER

A chosen card finds itself by turning over in mid air.

YOU WILL NEED
★ Any card deck.

1 Find a chosen card (see page 36). Tell your audience that you are going to make the chosen card flip itself over, and while you are doing this, secretly cut the card to the top of the deck.

2 Holding the deck in your left hand, bring your right hand over the cards. While you are doing this, push the top card slightly to the right with your left thumb.

3 With your right hand, lift the deck up, then throw it straight down into your left hand.

4 Your audience will be amazed as the chosen card flips over in mid air, and then lands on top of the deck!

FACING FACTS

Turn a chosen card face up behind your back!

YOU WILL NEED
★ Tapered cards from kit.
★ A Volunteer.

1 Shuffle all the cards together thoroughly. making sure all tapered ends are at the same end.

2 Fan out the cards and allow your volunteer to select a card. Whilst they look at it, turn the pack 180°.

3 Allow your volunteer to replace the card anywhere they like in the pack. Give the pack a quick shuffle, just to prove you have no idea where their card is.

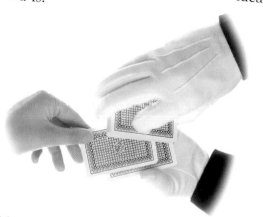

4 Hold the cards behind your back and strip out the chosen card. Flip it upside down, and bring the pack round to the front. When you spread the cards on the table, their chosen card will be face up among the rest of the deck.

JACKS BE NIMBLE

YOU WILL NEED
★ Tapered cards from kit.
★ A Volunteer.

It'll be Jumpin' Jack Flash when all four jacks exit the deck!

1 Before you begin, remove all Jacks from the deck, and make sure all tapered ends are at the same end, then turn the Jacks around, and put them back at different places through the deck.

2 Shuffle all the cards, and show your audience that all the Jacks are positioned randomly throughout the pack.

3 Hold the cards behind your back, and strip out the Jacks. While you do this, tell your audience a story about the Jacks; maybe that they all wanted to go out for the day, and planned a secret outing without telling anybody.

4 While you do this, quickly put the Jacks in your back pocket or up your sleeve. Then, when you bring the pack round to the front, all the Jacks will be missing! You can then pull them from your pocket to the amazment of your audience!

45

FEEL THE FORCE

You force someone to choose the card that you want them to.

1 The card which you will force someone to choose is at the bottom of the deck, so before you begin the trick, take a secret look at that card and remember it.

2 Tell a volunteer from your audience that you will force them to choose a card – name the card from the bottom of the deck. Hold the cards in your left hand, and place your right hand on top of them, with your right thumb underneath.

3 With the fingers of your right hand, move the cards back a few at a time. Ask your volunteer to say 'stop' at any time while you are doing this.

4 Pull back all the cards you have moved with your right hand. At the same time, drag the bottom card with your right thumb so that it is underneath the cards in your right hand. Hold up these cards to show the bottom one – it is, of course the card which you told your audience you would find in step 2 on page 46.

MIND READING

Baffle your audience by reading someone's mind - but it's all really down to some tricky sleight of hand!

1 Before you begin this trick, put any two cards into your trouser pocket.

2 Ask a member of your audience to shuffle a deck of cards. Deal the top three cards face up onto the table.

3 Look at the cards and memorise them. Then ask your volunteer to think of one of the cards on the table, but not to tell anyone. Pick up the cards, remembering the order they are in, and carefully put them on top of the other two cards already in your pocket.

4 Tell your audience that you know which card your volunteer is thinking of. Take out the two cards which you hid in your pocket before you began the trick – the audience will think that you only have one card left in your pocket, but you know you still have three. Return these two cards to the deck without showing their faces.

5 Ask your volunteer to name their card. Reach into your pocket, and because you memorised the order that you put the cards in, you are able to pull out the chosen card with a flourish. Your audience will think that you are an amazing mind reader!

MEGA MIND READING

What's better than reading one person's mind? Reading two, of course!

1 Prepare your trick. Take any card, and on its back put one pencil dot in the top left-hand and bottom right-hand corners. Put this card in your pocket until you are ready to use it.

2 Shuffle the deck of cards, then ask two volunteers to select a card each, which they need to remember without telling anyone.

3 While they are remembering their cards, secretly retrieve the marked card from your pocket and put it on the bottom of the deck.

4 Ask one of your volunteers to replace their card on top of the deck. Cut the deck. Place the top half of cards in your left hand, then put the other half on top. The marked card is now on top of the first chosen card.

5 Spread the deck face down to find your marked card. Cut the deck in half one card below the marked card, then put the top half of cards underneath the other half. This takes the first chosen card to the bottom of the deck, with the marked card above it. Quickly look at the bottom card and remember it.

6 Ask your second volunteer to replace their card on the top of the deck. Cut the deck as you did in step 4 on page 51 to bring the first and second chosen cards and the marked card together.

7 Announce to your audience that you will now read your first volunteer's mind! Make a big show of concentrating hard, closing your eyes and breathing deeply. Then reveal the name of the chosen card (which you found out in step 5 on page 52) ask your volunteer to confirm that this is the right one, and your audience will gasp!

8 They will be even more amazed when you complete the trick and read a second person's mind. To do this, spread the pack of cards in front of you. The second chosen card will be on top of the first chosen card. Of course, now that you know the secret of how to read two minds at once, there's no reason why you can't read three, four or even five!

THREE'S COMPANY

Link three randomly selected cards together in the middle of a deck!

YOU WILL NEED
★ Tapered cards from kit.
★ 3 Volunteers.

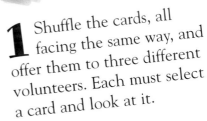

1 Shuffle the cards, all facing the same way, and offer them to three different volunteers. Each must select a card and look at it.

2 While your volunteers are looking at their cards, reverse your deck.

3 Allow each volunteer to replace their card randomly into the deck.

4 Hold the cards behind your back, and strip out the chosen three. Keeping them all together, cut the deck in half and place them in the middle.

5 Bring the deck back round to view, and fan it out. When you turn it over, ask your volunteers to take back their cards. They will be together.

BACK-TO-BACK

You show your audience two cards and hold them face-to-face. When you blow on them, they are suddenly back-to-back!

1 Hold a card in each hand by its side between your thumb and first finger – the faces should be opposite each other. Now position your hands about 12 in. (30 cm) apart.

2 Bring your hands together until each card can be gripped by the thumb and second finger of the opposite hand. There should be a gap of about 1/2 in. (1 cm) between the cards.

3 Raise the cards toward your mouth and tell your audience that you will blow between them, and they will magically change places.

4 As soon as you have blown between the cards, start to move your hands back to their original positions 12 in. (30 cm) apart, the right hand taking the left card, the left hand taking the right card.

5 This trick needs a lot of practice before you perform it. Start slowly and gradually build up speed until you can make the exchange without hesitation. It is the smoothness of your move which will fool your audience.

IT'S MAGIC

The cards are now magically back-to-back

FIVE-WAY SPLIT

This trick uses a more complicated method to find a chosen card.

1 Preparation is key to the success of this trick. Before your show, take all the diamonds from your deck of cards. Count out a pile of thirty-five cards – put five diamonds underneath the pile and five on top.

2 Give the deck of cards to a member of the audience, and ask them to deal the cards into five piles, face down on the table. Ask them to pick a card from the middle of one of the piles. They need to remember it and can show it to the audience, but you must not see what it is.

3 Tell your volunteer to put the card face down on top of any of the piles, then ask them to put the piles together to make one deck of cards. Cut the pack several times to make sure their card is well mixed with the others.

4 Spread the deck of cards. To find the right card, scan slowly over the cards. The chosen card will be between two diamonds, so as soon as you see a card splitting two diamonds, you know you have found the right one.

VANISHING ACE

Make an Ace disappear - and then appear somewhere else, by magic!

YOU WILL NEED
★ Any card deck.
★ 2 volunteers.

1 Secretly hide the Ace of Diamonds in a place near to where you will perform.

2 Show the other Aces to your audience, holding them so that only the tip of the Ace of Hearts is showing. Point out to your audience that you are holding the Ace of Clubs, the Ace of Diamonds and the Ace of Spades, and that you are going to make the Ace of Diamonds disappear.

3 Turn the cards over and return them to the deck in different places. Shuffle the cards yourself, or pass them to a volunteer to shuffle them.

4 Invite someone from the audience to take out the Ace of Diamonds. It's not there!

5 Now ask someone else to go to the hiding place. Surprise! There is the missing Ace.

MAGIC TOUCH

Here is a really impressive way of naming cards just by touching them.

1 Before your show, take one card from your deck and put it in your back pocket. Remember what was on the card.

2 Ask a member of your audience to shuffle the deck of cards for you. Take the deck face down behind your back, and put the hidden card face up on top. While you are doing this, pretend to the audience that you are reading the card by touch.

3 Bring the deck out from behind your back, holding it in front of you so that your audience can see the face of the card you placed on top of the deck. Name the card for the audience.

4 While you are doing this, look at the card in front of you, which is actually on the bottom of the deck, and remember it.

63

5 Take the deck behind your back again. Remove the card from the bottom of the deck, and place it face up on top of the card which you have just named, all the time telling your audience that you are guessing which card it is by touch alone.

6 You can now bring the cards forward and name the next card. At the same time, remember the new card on the bottom of the deck, so that you can perform the trick all over again!